Buyer's Guide to United States Gold Coins

By Q. David Bowers

Foreword by David W. Akers
U.S. Gold Coin Survey by Richard A. Bagg, Ph.D

BOWERS AND MERENA GALLERIES, INC.
Publications Department
Box 1224
Wolfeboro, New Hampshire 03894
©1989 by Bowers and Merena Galleries, Inc.
All rights reserved.

Portions of the text appeared in "The Monthly Summary" of *The Coin Dealer Newsletter* in 1987.

The following members of the Bowers and Merena Galleries staff assisted as follows: Linda Heilig, layout; Cathy W. Dumont, photographs; Richard A. Bagg, Ph.D. and Andrew W. Pollock III, research.

Contents

	Foreword	9
	Introduction	13
	Uncirculated U.S. Gold Coin Survey	17
1	Gold Coins: Their History	23
2	Gold Dollars	33
3	Quarter Eagles	43
4	Three-Dollar Gold Pieces	59
5	Stellas	65
6	Half Eagles	69
7	Eagles	87
8	Double Eagles	101
9	Summary	117
	Bibliography	119
	Index	121

FOREWORD

Foreword

By David W. Akers

Coins have been minted in a variety of metals almost from the time they first came into general usage over two thousand years ago. Of course, coins have been struck in such common metals as copper, nickel, brass, aluminum, and even pewter. They have been made of precious metals such as silver, gold and platinum. And they have even been minted in such exotic or lesser known metals as palladium and electrum. But it can be safely stated that gold coins have always held the position of greatest importance in the minds of collectors and the general public as well.

United States gold coins, first issued for circulation in 1795 and last minted in 1933, are aesthetically among the most beautiful coins ever minted by any country. From the early designs of Robert Scot to the masterpieces of design of the famous artist and sculptor, Augustus Saint-Gaudens, U.S. gold coins offer an intriguing variety of styles. Since they were struck at seven different U.S. mints, and were minted from gold mined in different regions of the country, U.S. gold coins also display a truly remarkable diversity of appearance. There are gold coins that are deep yellow in color, others with a distinctive pink or coppery hue, still others with an obvious greenish cast. The quality of minting also varied widely from mint to mint and year to year, and virtually every U.S. gold coin issue has its own unique, distinctive characteristics, its "fingerprints" so to speak, that distinguish it from other issues. For instance, an 1854-D half eagle looks decidedly different from an 1854 Philadelphia coin, which in turn is unlike an 1854-S, and a person that is aware of these differences can tell which is which without even turning the coin over to look at the mintmark!

Despite their popularity with collectors ever since collecting coins first became fashionable in this country in the 1850s, U.S. gold coins were not widely researched and written about until the 1960s. Even today, there has been relatively little written on the subject, and every one of the six U.S. gold coin series still offers nearly endless possibilities for original research and both interesting and potentially profitable discoveries.

In no other areas of U.S. coinage are the traditionally used mintage figures less accurate for determining the true rarity of a given issue. Many issues with rather high mintages are extremely rare, while others with much smaller mintages are comparatively common. Consider the case of the 1823 and 1828 half eagles. The mintage of the 1823 is only half that of the 1828 and yet the 1828 is at least five times as rare.

Absolute rarity (the total number of existing specimens) is only one half of the rarity equation. The other half is condition rarity, that is, the rarity of a particular issue in high grade, especially the various stages of Uncirculated condition. Here is another area that has only recently been studied, and it is full of surprises.

There are many U.S. gold coin issues that are easily obtainable in lower grades or even minimal Uncirculated condition but that are either unobtainable or extremely rare in higher Mint State grades. Again using the extensive half eagle series as an example, consider the 1911-S Indian Head. This issue has the second highest mintage figure for the series and can be easily found in EF or AU condition. In choice or gem Mint State, however, it is extremely rare, one of the four or five rarest of the entire series. In gem condition, for example, it is perhaps eight to 10 times as rare as the 1908-S which has a mintage figure that is only 6% as great as that of the 1911-S! What is the reason for this? No one really knows for sure, but perhaps further dedicated research could uncover the reason.

The possibilities for study and discovery in the U.S. gold series are nearly limitless. One could literally spend a lifetime studying the different issues and still learn something new almost every day. Q. David Bowers' *Buyer's Guide to United States Gold Coins* is the perfect place to start that study and it will point the way to many possible avenues of interest where further research can lead to exciting discoveries.

INTRODUCTION

Introduction

Welcome to the *Buyer's Guide to United States Gold Coins*. This compact volume is intended to achieve two purposes:

First, I give an overview of United States gold coins, the various denominations from $1 to $20, how they were produced, and how they were distributed. The distribution is particularly important, as it influences the availability of gold coins in certain grades today.

Second, I provide information concerning which areas of gold coins, and which varieties in particular, seem to be undervalued in today's market: undervalued in relation to common or "type" pieces. It is often the case that a coin which sells for 10% to 20% more than a common or "type" issue may be 50 times or even 100 times rarer! Obviously, the purchase of such "sleepers" provides the potential for attractive profits in the future.

An example of such profits—perhaps an extreme example—but certainly quite an impressive one, is provided by an 1864-S $5 piece which appeared in the Norweb Collection Sale in October 1987. Described as Lot 875, the piece was featured in the catalogue as follows:

> 1864-S MS-64 or finer. A superb coin, well struck, and very frosty, from the Thomas G. Melish Collection, and possibly the only Uncirculated specimen known to exist. The Melish coin is the only piece recorded in

David Akers' survey. The Eliasberg Collection coin, sold by us in October 1982, had an EF-40 obverse and a VF-30 reverse.

The obtaining of an Uncirculated example of the 1864-S half eagle in your lifetime may well be predicated upon your success in acquiring Lot 875.

Although it is redundant to mention here, the desirability of the Uncirculated piece is accented by the fact that no AU pieces were recorded by David Akers, and only a handful of lesser condition examples are known.

By way of further background information, I mention that the coin had appeared in Abe Kosoff's sale of the Thomas G. Melish Collection in 1956, was purchased by New Netherlands Coin Company, and was sold into the Norweb Collection for the price of $75. A number of years later, David Akers, whose research I will be referring to a number of times in the following text, studied the appearance of gold coins at auction, and published his findings in a series of volumes, one devoted to each gold coin denomination. Under the category of the 1864-S $5 piece, the only Uncirculated coin he was able to locate in his study was the Melish piece. When Louis Eliasberg was assembling his unprecedented collection of American gold coins, the finest 1864-S he was able to locate was in a circulated grade.

A glance at the *A Guide Book of United States Coins*, the 1989 edition, states that for this variety 3,888 were minted, and that examples are valued at $1,000 in VF-20 grade, $2,200 in EF-40 grade, and $3,000 in AU-50 grade. Uncirculated examples are not priced.

If I don't state another word, at this point you know that at $3,000 an AU-50 specimen would indeed be a good buy, for if you were to acquire such a piece, you would have a coin of which no comparable example has crossed the auction block in years.

What is an Uncirculated 1864-S worth? That question went through the minds of many bidders in our Norweb Collection Sale. Prior to the auction we received a number of telephone inquiries from prospective bidders. One client indicated that he would bid in the $10,000 range, certainly a generous figure, and a price more than three times the AU-50 listing in the *Guide Book*. Then another client indicated the worth at $15,000. As the sale approached, additional bidders got into the act, and it was evident that at the sale the coin would bring over $20,000, perhaps even

$30,000. As it turns out, all of these estimates and ideas were remote from what actually happened. A fantastic skirmish of bidders ensued in the packed auction gallery, and the price soared to $110,000!

The point of this is that, prior to the sale, had you asked a dealer about an Uncirculated 1864-S, you might have learned that the piece was indeed scarce, perhaps even rare, but not much attention would have been paid to it. However, properly described in an auction catalogue, with its true rarity pointed out, the coin amazed onlookers and brought a sum equivalent to a small fortune. Honorable and Mrs. R. Henry Norweb had the foresight to acquire the coin for $75 in 1956, paying at the time more than any other numismatists were willing to spend for it. Their judgment was validated by the fact that, when sold, their $75 investment brought more than 1,400 times the original cost! I wonder if in any other investment medium anywhere else in the world, a comparable figure could be found?

While I do not suggest that gold coins purchased today are going to return 1,400 times your investment a few decades from now, I do suggest and strongly believe that there are many fantastic opportunities for alert buyers to acquire pieces which will show a nice profit.

The present book incorporates my ideas together with those of certain Bowers and Merena Galleries staff members. I suggest that you use the book in combination with other information, such as pricing guides and references on the subject of gold coins. In the latter category, you may find my *U.S. Gold Coins: An Illustrated History* book to be useful. This volume was produced in 1982 and is illustrated with coins from the fabulous Eliasberg Collection. I also highly recommend David Akers' studies of gold coins.

Portions of the following text appeared in the "Monthly Summary" section of *The Coin Dealer Newsletter* in the autumn of 1987.

Investigate the area of sleepers among United States gold coins. An interesting challenge awaits you, and the potential for an attractive profit is certainly there!

Q. David Bowers—February 9, 1989

INTRODUCTION

Uncirculated U.S. Gold Coin Survey
1838-1933
Some Technical Considerations
By Richard A. Bagg, Ph.D.

Forming a collection of United States gold coins can be a rewarding and challenging experience. Whether you are attempting to build a beautiful type set, or a collection of a specific denomination by date and mintmark varieties, you may find that many years elapse between public offerings of truly Uncirculated (MS-60 or finer) specimens, a situation which is particularly true in the case of rarer issues. In the past, a collection which combines the characteristics of rarity and high condition has proven to be an outstanding financial investment.

In an effort to access the true rarity of United States gold coins in Uncirculated grade, I have found the following sources to be useful in the determination of "sleeper" issues, coins which in Uncirculated grade are very rare, often much rarer than perceived by the public:

Walter Breen's monographs on gold coins, published by Hewitt Brothers in the 1960s, mark one of the earliest attempts to describe the rarity of various United States gold issues. Although these volumes, which range from gold dollars through selected varieties of $10 pieces, are primarily a study of minute die varieties, sufficient mention is made of significant coins and rarity in certain grades to merit inclusion in the present study. For example, in his reference to the 1870-CC half eagle, Walter Breen makes the notation, "None even approaching Extremely Fine," which at once signifies that it is a "sleeper" in higher grades and, to the knowledge of that writer is nonexistent in Uncirculated preservation. Since Walter Breen's monographs were published many other studies have been made, some obsoleting his pioneer efforts, but still they remain valuable in the present time.

In 1971 Don Taxay, in his *Encyclopedia of United States Coins*, provided notations regarding the rarity of United States gold issues. Such terms as "extremely rare," meaning one to three known, "very rare," meaning seven to nine known, and so on were employed. The 1976 edition of this work, the latest edition published, continued the philosophy. Although this valuable book is now out of print, his work has proven very useful for collectors and researchers alike.

Beginning in 1975 and continuing until 1982, David W. Akers published a series of separate monographs covering various United States gold denominations from the dollar through the double eagle. Surveying actual auction records, the author sought to quantify existing rare issues while at the same time mathematically formulating an "average grade" for each issue. The availability of specific issues was determined by counting the total number of appearances and dividing this number by the total number of catalogues surveyed. Thus, an example which appeared in 8% of the sales surveyed can be considered rare for, by implication, 92% of the auction sales lacked the variety. The study did not delete repetitious offerings, so the same specimen of a coin offered multiple times over a period of years gave a somewhat inflated rating for certain issues, a factor which, to an extent, is present in the research of other authors, including the present writers. In 1988 the same author produced another book, *A Handbook of 20th Century Gold Coins* which provided a valuable study of the Pratt and Saint-Gaudens coinages.

Another effort to study the rarity of coins was developed by

Andrew W. Pollock, III, of the Bowers and Merena staff, whereby a pedigree index for each variety, in instances in which coins can be verified by illustration or detailed descriptions, has been substituted for auction appearances. This research is quite meaningful. For example, although there have been 12 auction offerings of the 1861-D gold dollar recorded in a particular survey since 1972, Pollock's *Numismatic Register* has broken this number down into just seven *different* specimens appearing.

Rome's Reports, and, more recently, Krause Publications have provided an annual edition of auction sales titled *Auction Prices Realized*. These sources provided exact locations in various auction sales for all United States gold issues and proved helpful in the present research for accessing the availability of Uncirculated specimens. No attempt was made to isolate repetitive offerings, and it may be the case that a given coin has appeared more than once over a period of years.

The approach of the present volume uses the aforementioned information and techniques, plus other data, to arrive at a relative approximation of known Uncirculated specimens for the United States gold series from 1838 to 1933. The data base consisted of the recent auction period from 1972 through 1988. Uncirculated examples of earlier U.S. gold coins, 1795 to 1837, are also discussed in the present volume, with the research dating back to appearances from an even earlier period.

The present survey treats only Uncirculated coins and not those in other grades. Auction appearances provide the main data base, although private transactions, when verified, are also considered. Rumored private transactions, external fixed price list data, and general numismatic articles are not covered in our survey; only public and verifiable information is included.

There are several sources of possible errors. The first lies with the nature of grading itself. Grading is an art more than a science, and it has been proven that two people can look at the same coin and come up with two different opinions. What one cataloguer might designate as MS-60, or an Uncirculated coin to be included in the present survey, another cataloguer may designate as AU-55, or a condition below the present field of study. In addition, the multiple appearances of the same coin at auction introduced errors. As noted, 12 auction appearances of an 1861-D gold dollar in Uncirculated grade were found upon study to represent just seven different coins. However, it is our belief that these factors fall evenly on coins in all series, so that the *relative* rarity is quite accurate. Thus, a coin which we designate as "AAA" is indeed significantly rarer in Uncirculated condition than one we designate as "A." This brings us to the notation system:

A United States gold coin which has not been offered in Uncirculated grade at auction during the 1972 to 1988 period is depicted a "AAAA." If one, two, or three appearances were noted, the coin was labeled "AAA"; four to six examples, "AA"; and seven to 12 examples, "A." A coin with over 12 offerings is labeled "B."

This information is presented in the form of charts. At a glance it can be noted, for example, that Carson City half eagles are virtually unobtainable in Uncirculated grade. It is also shown that New Orleans double eagles in this grade are exceedingly rare. San Francisco $10 pieces from the period 1854 through the 1860s are nearly impossible to acquire in Uncirculated grade, and an auction sale of one of these specimens would prove to be a significant numismatic event. Many other analyses of these charts are possible.

The reader of this book who is confronted with the possibility of acquiring a coin which we rate as "AAAA," in other words a piece we have not noted as appearing at auction during the period studied, knows that here is a major opportunity, perhaps a once in a lifetime event. We hasten to add that no team of researchers can know all things, and possibly specimens may have changed hands in private transactions, or in obscure auction sales not surveyed, or may lay unidentified in hoards. However, at the very least a specimen coming on the market, and a category which we presently designate as "AAAA," is a great rarity, and it even may be unique.

The present study is the first time such detailed information has been available in a single volume, and it is offered as a beginning for research yet to come by ourselves and other writers. This survey of "sleeper" specimens points to one of the secrets of successful coin buying: that is, a combination of exquisite beauty, Uncirculated grade, and extreme rarity can be financially and personally rewarding.

There is no substitute for knowledge, and it is the hope of the present compilers that this volume will contribute measurably to your knowledge on the subject of Uncirculated coin rarity.

The Notation System

A United States gold coin which has not been offered in Uncirculated grade at auction during the 1972 to August 1988 period is depicted a "AAAA." If one, two, or three appearances were noted, the coin was labeled "AAA"; four to six examples, "AA"; and seven to 12 examples, "A." A coin with over 12 offerings is labeled "B."

CHAPTER ONE

Gold Coins: Their History

In numismatics, as in other walks of life, knowledge is closely equated with success. The more you know, the more successful you will be. The field of gold coins is no exception.

Whether you endeavor to pick up a few scattered "sleepers" as a potential investment, or whether you are determined to acquire a date run or a set of coins, you will find background information concerning the creation and distribution of gold coins to be of value. Beyond that, in the pages to follow there are specific suggestions for identifying undervalued scarce and rare pieces. But, first, here is a survey of United States gold coins:

Gold has always fascinated mankind, and today the lure is no less than it was in the last century when the prospect of acquiring the bright yellow metal was responsible for the California Gold Rush. Silver has its advocates, platinum may be worth more from time to time on the market, but it is gold that has been characterized as the most noble of metals, the king of elements, the stuff of which dreams and treasures are made.

From the very outset, gold was conceived as a part of the federal coinage system. However, when the Philadelphia Mint opened its doors in 1792 and began producing coins in quantity for circulation in 1793, no gold pieces were among the issues struck. It was required that surety bonds in the amount of $10,000 each be posted by key Mint officials, and they were unable to raise the sum. So, the advent of gold coins awaited the year 1795, by which time the bond amounts were reduced and the requirements satisfied. The first United States gold coinage consisted of $5 pieces, called half eagles, delivered that year, followed by $10 or eagle pieces. An additional denomination, the $2½ piece or quarter eagle, had its advent in 1796, thus completing the spectrum of early United States gold coin denominations.

The country was in its fledgling state, and in the channels of commerce, both within the United States and abroad, there was a great distrust of paper money (previously-issued Continental Currency notes were virtually worthless, so obligations of the new American government were viewed with suspicion), and emphasis was on intrinsic value. So, framers of the act passed on April 2, 1792 took care that the weights of gold and other coins were equal to their intrinsic or melt-down value. The gold $10 piece was established at a weight of 270 grains, consisting of nine parts gold and 10 parts copper, the copper being added to give strength to the alloy. Lesser denominations, the $5 and $2½ values, were given proportional weights.

The intrinsic value concept was quite satisfactory so far as promoting the acceptance of new federal coins, but a backlash occurred whenever the value of gold metal rose on international markets. Each time this happened, vast quantities of minted quarter eagles, half eagles, and $10 pieces went into the hands of bullion brokers who melted or exported them.

As published mintage figures in the *Guide Book* reveal, quarter eagles were produced in low quantities during the early years. $10 pieces were also coined in relatively modest amounts, with relatively few exceptions, with production in the early years terminating in 1804, after which no pieces were minted until 1838. Thus it fell upon the $5 half eagle to be the "workhorse" denomination. Gold coins of this value were struck more or less continuously from 1795 onward, with typical years generating production in the tens of thousands of pieces. In 1810 a record 100,287 coins were produced, and the next year, 1811, the mintage was about the same and amounted to 99,581. A glance at the figures in the *Guide Book* will show generous mintages of half eagles through the 1820s and early 1830s. At the same time, it will be readily observed that these pieces, which by superficial glance should be "common," post some of the highest values in the American series. Then there is the curious notation that although 17,796 half eagles were minted in 1822, just three are known. An example in EF-40 grade, catalogued by the present writer for the sale of the Eliasberg Collection of U.S. Gold Coins in 1982, realized $687,500!

The explanation is provided by the bullion markets of the time. The price of gold rose during the 1820s and early 1830s, so that by the end of the period very few pieces had escaped the melting pot. A freshly-minted 1822 half eagle, or any other half eagle of the era, could be melted down and return more than $5 in value. Producing such coins was an exercise in futility for the Mint. Realizing this, Congress passed legislation on June 28, 1834, effective August 1, 1834, mandating a change in the authorized weight of gold coins. After that time, gold coins were worth less in melt-down value than face value, so they were once again seen in the channels of circulation.

Until the 1820s, there was no significant known source of native gold in the United States. Bullion to make quarter eagles, half eagles, and eagles came from a variety of origins, including foreign gold coins melted down (an important source), bullion from Central and South America, and the reduction of various wrought items such as jewelry. By the 1820s, gold discoveries in North Carolina became important. In 1838 mints were established at Dahlonega, Georgia and Charlotte, North Carolina, to produce coins from bullion found in those areas.

From August 1, 1834 through the late 1840s, gold coins were produced in fair quantities at Philadelphia, then subsequently in Charlotte, Dahlonega, and the additional branch mint at New Orleans. Supplies of gold primarily came from Georgia and North Carolina, with additional amounts coming from international payments, the melting down of foreign coins, and other traditional sources.

In the United States, gold coins were commonly used in large commercial transactions. At the time, during the middle of the 19th century, the country was inundated with a flood of privately-issued paper currency notes, with most values being from $1 to $10, but with abundant quantities of values from $20 to $100 as well, plus some stray examples of higher denominations. Just about every bank in existence issued its own currency. The enforcement of laws was loose, and many were the so-called "wildcat banks" which had little or no substantive backing, but which issued hundreds of thousands of dollars in worthless notes. The public distrusted these notes, and many demanded gold in payment for transactions. On the international scene, privately issued bank notes were not accepted, and gold coins were the norm. Thus, quantities of United States gold coins found their way to England, France, and other trading centers.

The discovery of gold at Sutter's Mill on the American River in California in January 1848 ignited the Gold Rush, which saw the migration westward of tens of thousands of individuals. Soon, vast quantities of gold were extracted from the rivers and soil of California. Shipped to the Eastern markets, the yellow metal became "common" in relation to earlier supplies. In view of the increased availability of gold, in 1849 two new coin denominations were created. The first was the gold dollar, which was to become the smallest federal gold coin. The second denomination was the $20 double eagle, minted in pattern form in 1849 and for general circulation beginning in 1850. This new, large, heavy coin made it economical to convert large amounts of bullion to struck form, for it took much less manpower and effort to make one double eagle than it did to coin an equivalent amount of gold in four $5 pieces or eight $2½ pieces. By 1853, gold had become so plentiful in relation to silver that silver had risen sharply on the market, and federal silver coins were worth more in bullion value than in face value—the same situation which confronted gold coins two decades earlier.

In the meantime, large quantities of gold came forth from California, and record numbers of coins were struck. In the year 1851, for example, the Philadelphia Mint saw a coinage of over two million double eagles, equal to over $40 million in face value.

It was not until 1861 that federal notes were made in quantity for circulation. During the 1850s the supply of privately issued bank notes grew sharply, and abuses of such issues continued. Gold coins continued to be the refuge for those distrustful of paper money. During the Civil War, the first federal "greenbacks" were issued, and in the South the Confederate States of America produced its own currency. The values of federal and Confederate paper money were uncertain, and at one point Union notes sold at a sharp discount in terms of coins. In other words, $1 in "hard money"—gold or silver coins—was worth more than a $1 note. Eventually, Confederate notes became worthless. After the Civil War ended, federal greenbacks and gold coins traded at par, although it was not until the 1870s that gold and silver coins were once again seen in general circulation. By about 1880, public faith in federal currency had been securely established, and no longer were $5, $10, $20, and other gold coins demanded for payment. By this time, privately-issued bank notes had disappeared from circulation. Federal currency became the mainstay for large transactions.

There was an exception, and the exception was provided by international trading. Foreign merchants and bankers were skeptical of United States paper money and often demanded gold. The memory was still clear of the depreciated value of federal notes during the Civil War and the eventual worthlessness of Confederate notes. London banks which had been paid in Confederate notes less than two decades earlier saw their investment become worth zero, and they weren't about to repeat the scenario.

In general, United States gold coins were widely used for commercial transactions in America from 1795 up until about 1880, for reasons stated, and after 1880 found their main use on the international market. This history and background has important implications for the rarity of gold coins as we perceive such today.

Gold coin production continued with intensity through the late 19th century. By that time North Carolina and Georgia sources of gold had largely petered out and production in California had diminished, but a new source, the Cripple Creek district of Colorado had been exploited and was yielding untold millions in yellow metal. Additional gold was obtained from other western sources, including Montana and Nevada. The San Francisco Mint, established in 1854 to convert California gold bullion into coins, remained an important mint. The Carson City Mint, established in 1870, continued in operation through 1885, then again from 1889 through 1893, then closed its doors. In 1906 a new mint, at Denver, Colorado, was opened and produced large quantities of gold coins, primarily from Cripple Creek metal.

Although today it is common to read that the United States was on the "gold standard" from 1795 onward, in actuality our country did not adopt the gold standard system until the year 1900, at which time the United States was one of the last developed nations to do so. Under the gold standard, countries participating in this stored gold coins and bullion in central banks and simply exchanged currency or certificates among themselves to settle transactions. Thus, after the year 1900 large quantities of American coins were stored in European, South American, and other vaults and were seldom moved. In the meantime, within the United States gold coins were rarely seen in day to day commerce.

If you had been a typical citizen in the year 1900, chances

are that during everyday grocery purchases, real estate transactions, and any other business transacted during a given 12-month period not a single gold coin would have been encountered, particularly if you lived in the East (gold coins were seen in circulation with more frequency in the West). Although gold issues were not needed in everyday circulation, they continued to be minted in record quantities. For example, the year 1904 saw a coinage of over six million double eagles at Philadelphia and over five million in San Francisco. What happened to them? Most were shipped overseas.

Gold coinage continued in large quantities, and in the 1920s, when gold coins were mainly kept in banks and rarely seen in circulation, record numbers were produced. The year 1928 saw a production of 8,816,000 double eagles, an all-time high!

From 1929 onward, the economic situation in the United States deteriorated, creating what eventually became known as the Great Depression. Unemployment increased, factory production decreased, and many banks, security firms, and others became bankrupt. By the time of the inauguration of President Franklin D. Roosevelt in 1933 there was widespread concern for the security of the American monetary system. On April 5, 1933, the new president proclaimed that gold coins were to be returned by the public to the Federal Reserve System by May 1st, with the exception of pieces of numismatic value. Citizens were prohibited from holding gold except for: "Such amounts of gold as may be required for legitimate and customary use in industry, professions or art within a reasonable time, including gold prior to refining and stocks of gold in reasonable amounts for the usual trade requirements of owners mining and refining such gold. Gold coins and gold certificates in an amount not exceeding in the aggregate of $100 belonging to any one person, and gold coins having a recognized special value to collectors of rare and unusual coins."

On December 28, 1933, the order was revised slightly, and, among other provisions, the statement allowing individuals to hold up to $100 worth of gold coins or gold certificates (in addition to pieces having recognized numismatic value) was deleted, after which only numismatic pieces could be legally held. In the same year the government issued several notices to the effect that the United States would remain on the gold standard and that citizens should not be alarmed.

The Gold Reserve Act of January 30, 1934 provided that: "No gold shall thereafter be coined, no gold coins shall hereafter be paid out or delivered by the United States . . . all gold coins in the United States shall be withdrawn from circulation . . . . " This legislation effectively ended gold coinage production and removed the gold backing of paper money. In the same year the United States withdrew from the gold standard.

At the time of the decrees of 1933 and 1934, millions of dollars worth of gold coins, primarily of the higher "bullion" values of $5, $10, and $20, were held by various world banks. The idea of shipping them back to the United States in exchange for currency seemed patently ridiculous to foreign bankers, especially in view of the increasing worthlessness of certain world currency at the time, as exemplified by German notes which weren't worth the paper they were printed on. Accordingly, foreign banks held on to United States gold coins more tightly than ever! Years later, when gold coin ownership regulations for United States citizens were relaxed, then dropped entirely, European, South American, and Asian banks became a prime source for specimens.

CHAPTER TWO

Gold Dollars

The gold dollar, measuring just 13mm in size, was envisioned as a useful article in commerce. Indeed, early issues in the series, from 1849 until the Civil War, fulfilled this purpose. While some pieces may have been hoarded, by and large most went into the channels of commerce where they saw ready use.

Today, collectors divide gold coins into major types:

Type I, designed by James B. Longacre (as were the other two types as well), bears on the obverse a compact head of Miss Liberty, quite similar to that used on the double eagle. Thirteen stars are around the border. The first year saw several varieties produced. Among Philadelphia Mint coins, certain 1849 gold dollars have a very small head and are considerably scarcer, although, except for a footnote in the *Guide Book*, this scarce style has created little attention. Later issues of 1849, and all others of the Type I issue through 1854, have a larger head. Certain early 1849 gold dollars made at the Philadelphia and Charlotte mints, and all of those made at Dahlonega and New Orleans, have an open wreath on the reverse. Later, the wreath was modified so that the terminal leaves are closer to the numeral 1, creating the so-called "closed wreath" style used through 1854.

GOLD DOLLAR: 1849-1854 Liberty Head

Designed by: James Barton Longacre
Issue dates: 1849-1854
Composition: 0.900 part gold, 0.100 part copper
Diameter: 13 mm
Weight: 25.8 grains
Edge: Reeded
Business strike mintage: 12,565,273
Proof mintage: Fewer than 50

Gold dollars of the Type I style were produced at four locations: Philadelphia, Charlotte, Dahlonega, and New Orleans. The Philadelphia Mint had the lion's share of production, mainly from gold shipped from California. In terms of quantities minted, New Orleans came next, with the Charlotte and Dahlonega mints finishing a distant third and fourth. In comparison to Philadelphia Mint production, which typically amounted to several million coins each year (in 1851, 1852, and 1853), the numbers minted at Charlotte and Dahlonega were almost negligible. Holding the record for low mintage of the Type I series is the 1854-D gold dollar, of which just 2,935 were minted.

In terms of availability today, Uncirculated examples of the Philadelphia Mint issues are occasionally seen, MS-63 pieces are scarce, and any Philadelphia Mint coin grading MS-65 or better by today's conservative interpretations can be deemed rare.

Branch mint coins are another story entirely. Nearly all known pieces show wear to one degree or another, and even MS-60 coins are rare.

A number of years ago, David W. Akers compiled auction appearances of United States golds coins from dollars through double eagles, and published the results in a series of books, one for each denomination. Anyone desirous of learning the relative rarity of any gold issue will find reading these books to be highly instructive. Although many coins have changed hands outside of the auction arena, and although grading interpretations have changed since the study was made, his findings remain highly relevant inasmuch as the *relative* rarities still remain in the same order. If anything, gold coins in higher grades, particularly Uncirculated, are much rarer today than the auction data suggest, for what cataloguers may have called Uncirculated five, ten, or twenty years ago is sometimes graded as AU today.

Type II gold dollars made their appearance part way through 1854. To facilitate handling by the public, the diameter of the gold dollar was increased from the earlier 13mm to a new

GOLD DOLLAR: 1854-1856 Indian Princess, Small Head

Designed by: James Barton Longacre
Issue dates: 1854-1856
Composition: 0.900 part gold, 0.100 part copper
Diameter: 15 mm
Weight: 25.8 grains
Edge: Reeded
Business strike mintage: 1,633,426
Proof mintage: Fewer than 50

GOLD DOLLAR: 1856-1889 Indian Princess, Large Head

Designed by: James Barton Longacre
Issue dates: 1856-1889
Composition: 0.900 part gold, 0.100 part copper
Diameter: 15 mm
Weight: 25.8 grains
Edge: Reeded
Business strike mintage: 5,327,363
Proof mintage: 8,700 (estimated)

standard of 15mm. The obverse motif was modified to the Indian Princess design. It soon developed that these pieces would not strike up well. The obverse portrait was in high relief, necessitating a strong metal flow to fill the deepest recesses of the die. At the same time, there was a metal requirement to fill in the date numerals and reverse inscription opposite the portrait in the dies. The result was that most dollars showed weakness in one area or another, typically at the two central numerals of the date. The Mint recognized this, and by 1856 discontinued the Type II, in favor of the new Type III design, with a shallower, modified portrait. However, some San Francisco Mint coins of the Type II motif were produced in the 1856 year.

Gold dollars of the Type II design are scarce today in all grades, particularly in view of the demand for them. Certain low mintage issues are rarities, with 1855-D, of which just 1,811 were made, taking high honors in this respect. In MS-60 grade, Philadelphia Mint coins are occasionally encountered. MS-63 pieces are scarce, and any coin with a legitimate claim to MS-65 or better is very rare. The Type II gold dollar is the key to a type set of this denomination and always has been in strong demand.

Type III gold dollars were minted in 1856 and continued through the end of the denomination in 1889. Those minted in the early part of the type production, from 1856 through the early Civil War, primarily found their way into circulation. As a result, MS-60 or finer specimens are scarce, and pieces grading MS-63 or better are rare. Some issues are more available than others, due to high mintages, with 1856, 1861, and 1862 having the highest production figures.

Beginning in the summer of 1862, gold and silver coins were hoarded, the government suspended payments of such coins into general circulation, and issues after this date were stored in Treasury vaults or exported. A glance at the mintage tables in the *Guide Book* will reveal that beginning in 1863 the mintage of the gold dollar denomination dropped sharply. From then through 1872 just a few thousand were produced each year. In the 1870s, payments of gold coins were again resumed by the government, and earlier-minted pieces were put into circulation. Today, all gold dollars of the 1863-1872 span are rare, and in higher grades they are extremely rare.

The years 1873 and 1874 saw an increased production of over 100,000 in each instance. It was the expectation of the government that the gold dollar would again be popular in commerce. However, this did not happen, gold dollars did not circulate widely, so beginning in 1875 mintages dropped sharply. From then through the end of the series relatively few were made.

Beginning around 1879, a popular passion for hoarding and speculating in gold dollars arose, and although the mintages were small, hundreds of pieces were set aside by investors and collectors. Thus, for gold dollars from 1879 through 1889 the low mintage figures must be tempered with an understanding of the long-ago penchant for hoarding. Although gold dollars of this span are scarce or even rare, they are not as rare as earlier issues of comparable low mintage. As one of a number of illustrations I could cite, take the 1879 gold dollar, of which 3,030 pieces were made; divided into 3,000 business strikes and 30 Proofs. I would estimate that today there are 500 or more Uncirculated pieces in existence. Several decades ago my firm handled two or three hundred of these, from a hoard that turned up in Baltimore.

Compare the 1879 gold dollar with the 1865. Of the 1865 gold dollar, 3,700 business strikes and 25 Proofs were made. If mintage figures alone were used as a criterion, one would assume that the 1879, with a lower business strike mintage, would be rarer. However, that is not the case, for the 1865 dollar was not saved by collectors or speculators at the time of issue. I estimate that fewer than 30 1865 gold dollars exist today in MS-63 or better grade.

Gold dollars are collected in two main ways today. The first and most popular is by design types. A type set consists of one of each of the three major styles. As noted, the Type II is the rarest. The second way is to acquire one of each date and mintmark variety. So far as straight dates and mintmarks are concerned, there are no "impossible" rarities, although the 1875 Philadelphia Mint issue is quite rare, and certain branch mint pieces, such as 1860-D and 1861-D, are likewise rarities.

In terms of value obtained for the price paid in the gold dollar series, there are many sleepers, inasmuch as rarities, particularly among higher grade Philadelphia Mint coins, are apt to be underpriced. Returning to my example of the 1865 gold dollar, in MS-60 grade the *Guide Book* lists it at $3,500, whereas the 1879, the other coin in my earlier example, catalogues at $1,750 in the same grade. Although the 1865 gold dollar catalogues for slightly over twice as much, it is at least a dozen times rarer.

Gold Dollars
1849-1889

	Philadelphia	Charlotte	Dahlonega	New Orleans	San Francisco
1849 Open Wreath	B	AAAA	B	B	—
1849 Closed Wreath	B	AA	—	—	—
1850	B	B	AA	B	—
1851	B	B	B	B	—
1852	B	B	AA	B	—
1853	B	B	AA	B	—
1854	B	—	AA	—	B
1855	B	AA	AAA	B	—
1856	B	—	AAA	—	A
1857	B	AA	AA	—	AAA
1858	B	—	A	—	B
1859	B	AA	B	—	AA
1860	B	—	A	—	B
1861	B	—	B	—	—
1862	B	—	—	—	—
1863	B	—	—	—	—
1864	B	—	—	—	—
1865	B	—	—	—	—
1866	B	—	—	—	—
1867	B	—	—	—	—
1868	B	—	—	—	—
1869	B	—	—	—	—
1870	B	—	—	—	B
1871	B	—	—	—	—
1872	B	—	—	—	—
1873	B	—	—	—	—
1874	B	—	—	—	—
1875	B	—	—	—	—
1876	B	—	—	—	—
1877	B	—	—	—	—
1878	B	—	—	—	—
1879	B	—	—	—	—
1880	B	—	—	—	—
1881	B	—	—	—	—
1882	B	—	—	—	—
1883	B	—	—	—	—
1884	B	—	—	—	—
1885	B	—	—	—	—
1886	B	—	—	—	—
1887	B	—	—	—	—
1888	B	—	—	—	—
1889	B	—	—	—	—

Explanatory Notes: B indicates more than 12 appearances in Uncirculated grade at public auction without regard to repetitious offerings, 1972-mid 1988; AAAA = 0 appearances; AAA = 1-3 appearances; AA = 4-6 appearances; A = 7-12 appearances; a dash indicates none minted.

CHAPTER THREE

Quarter Eagles

Quarter eagles were first made in 1796. Production was intermittent from that time through the last year of the series, 1929.

Early quarter eagles of the 1796-1834 style are rarities in each instance, although none is impossibly rare. Over the years a number of specialists have put together one of each date and major variety. As a perusal of the *Guide Book* listings will indicate, the series is punctuated by a number of key issues. Collecting the early series can be accomplished in one of several ways. The most popular is by design types, a procedure which necessitates obtaining the following issues: 1796 Capped Bust to Right, no obverse stars; 1796-1807 Capped Bust to Right, with obverse stars; 1808 Capped Bust to Left, large size; and 1821-1834 Capped Head to Left. Of these types the 1796 without stars and the 1808 are the most elusive and expensive.

By 1834, the price of gold metal on the bullion market had risen to the point at which quarter eagles and other gold denominations could be melted down at a profit. As a result, most earlier mintages were destroyed. Although production figures of early quarter eagles were sufficiently low that the pieces would be scarce in any event, today the mintage figures

QUARTER EAGLE: 1796 No Obverse Stars

Designed by: Robert Scot
Issue date: 1796
Composition: 0.9167 part gold, 0.0833 part copper
Diameter: 20 mm
Weight: 67.5 grains
Edge: Reeded
Business strike mintage: 963 (estimated)
Proof mintage: None

QUARTER EAGLE: 1796-1807 Capped Bust, Obverse Stars

Designed by: Robert Scot
Issue dates: 1796-1807
Composition: 0.9167 part gold, 0.0833 part copper
Diameter: 20 mm
Weight: 67.5 grains
Edge: Reeded
Business strike mintage: 18,524
Proof mintage: None

QUARTER EAGLE: 1808 Capped Bust to Left

Designed by: John Reich
Issue date: 1808
Composition: 0.9167 part gold, 0.0833 part copper
Diameter: 20 mm
Weight: 67.5 grains
Edge: Reeded
Business strike mintage: 2,710
Proof mintage: None

QUARTER EAGLE: 1821-1834 Capped Head to Left

Designed by: John Reich
Issue dates: 1821-1834
Composition: 0.9167 part gold, 0.0833 part copper
Diameter: 18.5 mm (1821-1827), 18.2 mm (1829-1834)
Weight: 67.5 grains
Edge: Reeded
Business strike mintage: 42,065
Proof mintage: Fewer than 150

QUARTER EAGLE: 1834-1839 Classic Head

Designed by: William Kneass
Issue dates: 1834-1839
Composition: 0.8992 part gold, 0.1008 part copper
Diameter: 18.2 mm
Weight: 64.5 grains
Edge: Reeded
Business strike mintage: 968,228
Proof mintage: Fewer than 50

QUARTER EAGLE: 1840-1907 Coronet

Designed by: Christian Gobrecht
Issue dates: 1840-1907
Composition: 0.900 part gold, 0.100 part copper
Diameter: 18 mm
Weight: 64.5 grains
Edge: Reeded
Business strike mintage: 11,921,171
Proof mintage: 4,232 (estimated)

tell only part of the story. The coins are even rarer than the low mintage figures suggest.

In 1834 the so-called Classic Head quarter eagle, of reduced weight, designed by William Kneass, appeared, the Classic Head style was produced from 1834 through 1839.

In 1840 the Coronet or Braided Hair quarter eagle appeared. This design, by Christian Gobrecht, was continued without interruption through the year 1907, the longest span in any American coinage series in which a major design was employed without substantial modification.

In 1908 a new design made its appearance: the innovative Indian Head motif by Bela Lyon Pratt. For the first time on an American coin, the designs were incuse on the coin, and the field or background of the coin, traditionally the lowest part of the design, was on this issue the highest. The Indian motif was produced from 1908 through 1915, then intermittently until 1929.

In terms of availability today, all pre-Classic Head quarters eagles, those minted from 1796 through 1834, are rare in any grade and are extremely rare in Uncirculated preservation.

Classic Head quarter eagles are scarce in higher grades and are rarities in Mint State. Particularly elusive are branch mint pieces.

Among Coronet or Braided Hair quarter eagles of the 1840-1907 type, a good rule of thumb is that issues from 1840 through the mid-1870s are available in worn grades in approximate proportion to their mintages. In Uncirculated grade nearly all are scarce, and many are extremely rare. The assembling of a complete set from 1840 onward, in MS-60 or better condition, is a practical impossibility.

For the astute buyer who takes time to study the series, there are many fantastic sleepers among earlier dates. Take, for example, the 1840 quarter eagle. The *Guide Book* suggests a price of $1,300 in MS-60 grade. One might think that, based upon this price, the coin would be more or less available. However, if you were to run advertisements in leading numismatic pub-

QUARTER EAGLE: 1908-1929 Indian

Designed by: Bela Lyon Pratt
Issue dates: 1908-1929
Composition: 0.900 part gold, 0.100 part copper
Diameter: 18 mm
Weight: 64.5 grains
Edge: Reeded
Business strike mintage: 7,250,261
Proof mintage: 1,827

lications and offer to pay ten times that price, or $13,000, for each and every MS-60 or better 1840 quarter eagle offered to you, I would be surprised if you could buy even a single piece! Skeptical? There is no need to be. A glance at David Akers' study shows that over a long span of years studied, *just two* Uncirculated 1840 quarter eagles came on the market, one in the Bell Collection in 1944 and one in the Kern Collection in 1950! To that survey can be added a piece we handled at auction a few years ago. It is quite possible that no more than three Uncirculated 1840 quarter eagles exist, and I am not even sure that there are that many, for the pieces sold years ago might not grade MS-60 by today's standards.

Quarter eagles after the mid-1870s underwent a different distribution pattern. Shortly after the time of minting, many were exported in payment for international transactions, with the result that European and South American banks, among others, accumulated quantities of them. In addition, quarter eagles became popular holiday gifts. Thus, American citizens set pieces aside. Although the assembly of a set of Uncirculated Coronet type quarter eagles from, say, 1880 onward, through 1907, would be a challenge, the coins are available, and over a period of a year or two such a collection could be completed.

Let me turn your attention to the 1904 quarter eagle. The *Guide Book* suggests a price of $1,100 for an MS-60 example. This price is not much different from the $1,300 suggested for the 1840 quarter eagle. However, several *thousand* MS-60 or better 1904 quarter eagles exist. While an Uncirculated 1904 quarter eagle is highly desirable, in view of the widespread demand for such pieces in date and type collections, it can hardly be called a rarity. My point is that, by comparison, the 1840 quarter eagle has to be one of the great sleepers of the century.

Lest you think that I studied hard to pick out the single example of a sleeper, I hasten to add that many other examples could be cited as well. In MS-60 or finer grade, probably fewer than a dozen examples exist of such otherwise "common" quarter eagle varieties as 1847-O, 1848, 1849, etc. In his study, David

Akers was able to locate just two Uncirculated 1860-S quarter eagles ever appearing on the market, and just a single 1861-S. The only 1861-S he was able to find came on the market in 1944, over 40 years ago! And yet the *Guide Book* lists the value of an 1861-S at just $1,200. One of my favorite sayings is and always has been, "Buy the book before the coin." By studying auction appearances of such coins as the 1861-S quarter eagle, and by reading specialized references on the series, you will learn what casual readers of the *Guide Book* don't know: that the 1861-S quarter eagle is so rare that if you could indeed buy one for $1,300 you could probably make a profit of $5,000 to $10,000 the next day!

Indian Head quarter eagles of the 1908-1929 type are mostly so-called common dates, except for the 1911-D issue, the lowest in the series, which is elusive in all grades. Modern grading interpretations, which are much stricter than those used a few years ago, are such that when Indian Head quarter eagles are re-evaluated using these new interpretations, a number of rarities emerge, even among the issues that are common in lower grades. For example, in MS-63 or finer grade, all issues from 1908 to 1915, the early range of the series, can be called rare, and in MS-65 condition they are extremely rare.

Quarter Eagles

	Philadelphia	Charlotte	Dahlonega
1838	B	AA	—
1839	B	AAA	AAA
1840	AAA	A	AAAA
1841	Proof Only	AAA	AAA
1842	AAAA	AAA	AAAA
1843 Small Date	—	AAA	AA
1843 Large Date	A	AAA	—
1844	AAA	AA	B
1845	B	—	AA
1846	AAA	AA	AA
1847	A	B	A
1848	A	AA	A
1848 CAL.	B	—	—
1849	A	AAA	AA
1850	B	AAA	AAA
1851	B	AAA	AAA
1852	B	AA	AAA
1853	B	—	AAA
1854	B	A	AAAA
1855	B	A	AAAA
1856	B	AA	AAA
1857	B	—	A
1858	B	A	—
1859	B	—	A
1860	B	AAA	—
1861	B	—	—
1862	B	—	—
1863	Proof Only	—	—
1864	AAAA	—	—
1865	AA	—	—
1866	AAA	—	—
1867	A	—	—
1868	A	—	—
1869	A	—	—
1870	AA	—	—
1871	A	—	—
1872	AAA	—	—
1873	B	—	—
1874	B	—	—
1875	AA	—	—
1876	B	—	—
1877	A	—	—
1878	B	—	—
1879	B	—	—
1880	B	—	—
1881	AA	—	—
1882	B	—	—

Explanatory Notes: B indicates more than 12 appearances in Uncirculated grade at public auction without regard to repetitious offerings, 1972-mid 1988; AAAA = 0 appearances; AAA = 1-3 appearances; AA = 4-6 appearances; A = 7-12 appearances; a dash indicates none minted.

1838-1882

	Denver	New Orleans	San Francisco
1838	—	—	—
1839	—	B	—
1840	—	AAA	—
1841	—	—	—
1842	—	AAA	—
1843 Small Date	—	B	—
1843 Large Date	—	A	—
1844	—	—	—
1845	—	AAA	—
1846	—	AA	—
1847	—	AA	—
1848	—	—	—
1848 CAL.	—	—	—
1849	—	—	—
1850	—	AAA	—
1851	—	A	—
1852	—	AA	—
1853	—	—	—
1854	—	B	AAAA
1855	—	—	—
1856	—	AAAA	A
1857	—	AA	AA
1858	—	—	—
1859	—	—	AA
1860	—	—	A
1861	—	—	AAA
1862	—	—	AAA
1863	—	—	AA
1864	—	—	—
1865	—	—	A
1866	—	—	AAA
1867	—	—	AAA
1868	—	—	AA
1869	—	—	AA
1870	—	—	AA
1871	—	—	B
1872	—	—	AAA
1873	—	—	AA
1874	—	—	—
1875	—	—	AA
1876	—	—	A
1877	—	—	B
1878	—	—	B
1879	—	—	AA
1880	—	—	—
1881	—	—	—
1882	—	—	—

Explanatory Notes: B indicates more than 12 appearances in Uncirculated grade at public auction without regard to repetitious offerings, 1972-mid 1988; AAAA = 0 appearances; AAA = 1-3 appearances; AA = 4-6 appearances; A = 7-12 appearances; a dash indicates none minted.

Quarter Eagles

	Philadelphia	Charlotte	Dahlonega
1883	B	—	—
1884	B	—	—
1885	B	—	—
1886	B	—	—
1887	B	—	—
1888	B	—	—
1889	B	—	—
1890	B	—	—
1891	B	—	—
1892	B	—	—
1893	B	—	—
1894	B	—	—
1895	B	—	—
1896	B	—	—
1897	B	—	—
1898	B	—	—
1899	B	—	—
1900	B	—	—
1901	B	—	—
1902	B	—	—
1903	B	—	—
1904	B	—	—
1905	B	—	—
1906	B	—	—
1907	B	—	—
1908	B	—	—
1909	B	—	—
1910	B	—	—
1911	B	—	—
1912	B	—	—
1913	B	—	—
1914	B	—	—
1915	B	—	—
1916	—	—	—
1917	—	—	—
1918	—	—	—
1919	—	—	—
1920	—	—	—
1921	—	—	—
1922	—	—	—
1923	—	—	—
1924	—	—	—
1925	—	—	—
1926	B	—	—
1927	B	—	—
1928	B	—	—
1929	B	—	—

Explanatory Notes: B indicates more than 12 appearances in Uncirculated grade at public auction without regard to repetitious offerings, 1972-mid 1988; AAAA = 0 appearances; AAA = 1-3 appearances; AA = 4-6 appearances; A = 7-12 appearances; a dash indicates none minted.

1883-1929

	Denver	New Orleans	San Francisco
1883	—	—	—
1884	—	—	—
1885	—	—	—
1886	—	—	—
1887	—	—	—
1888	—	—	—
1889	—	—	—
1890	—	—	—
1891	—	—	—
1892	—	—	—
1893	—	—	—
1894	—	—	—
1895	—	—	—
1896	—	—	—
1897	—	—	—
1898	—	—	—
1899	—	—	—
1900	—	—	—
1901	—	—	—
1902	—	—	—
1903	—	—	—
1904	—	—	—
1905	—	—	—
1906	—	—	—
1907	—	—	—
1908	—	—	—
1909	—	—	—
1910	—	—	—
1911	B	—	—
1912	—	—	—
1913	—	—	—
1914	B	—	—
1915	—	—	—
1916	—	—	—
1917	—	—	—
1918	—	—	—
1919	—	—	—
1920	—	—	—
1921	—	—	—
1922	—	—	—
1923	—	—	—
1924	—	—	—
1925	B	—	—
1926	—	—	—
1927	—	—	—
1928	—	—	—
1929	—	—	—

Explanatory Notes: B indicates more than 12 appearances in Uncirculated grade at public auction without regard to repetitious offerings, 1972-mid 1988; AAAA = 0 appearances; AAA = 1-3 appearances; AA = 4-6 appearances; A = 7-12 appearances; a dash indicates none minted.

CHAPTER FOUR

Three Dollar Gold Pieces

The reason for the production of the $3 piece is clouded in obscurity today. Suggestions advanced include the usefulness of the denomination to purchase 3-cent stamps in sheets of 100, and the possibility to buying 3-cent coins easily in the same quantity.

Of all gold denominations produced over a period of time, the $3 series is the least complex. Just one major design type was made, the Indian Princess motif by James B. Longacre. Coins of this style were produced continuously from 1854 through 1889. A variation is provided by the year 1854, all coins of which have the word DOLLARS in smaller letters on the reverse.

The original distribution pattern, which provides the key to understanding the rarity of pieces in certain grades today, is the same for $3 as for the previously-discussed $1 coins. Specimens were made for general use in circulation up to and including the Civil War. Beginning with the Civil War, mintages were reduced, and pieces produced were stored in Treasury vaults or exported, to be released in circulation in the 1870s, when gold payments were again resumed. In 1874 and again

$3 GOLD: 1854-1889 Indian Princess

Designed by: James Barton Longacre
Issue dates: 1854-1889
Composition: 0.900 part gold, 0.100 part copper
Diameter: 20.5 mm
Weight: 77.4 grains
Edge: Reeded
Business strike mintage: 538,074
Proof mintage: 2,060 (estimated)

Three Dollar Gold
1854-1889

	Philadelphia	Dahlonega	New Orleans	San Francisco
1854	B	AA	AA	—
1855	B	—	—	AA
1856	B	—	—	A
1857	B	—	—	AAA
1858	A	—	—	—
1859	B	—	—	—
1860	B	—	—	AAA
1861	B	—	—	—
1862	B	—	—	—
1863	B	—	—	—
1864	B	—	—	—
1865	A	—	—	—
1866	B	—	—	—
1867	B	—	—	—
1868	B	—	—	—
1869	B	—	—	—
1870	B	—	—	AAAA
1871	B	—	—	—
1872	B	—	—	—
1873 Closed 3	AA	—	—	—
1873 Open 3	Proof Only	—	—	—
1874	B	—	—	—
1875	Proof Only	—	—	—
1876	Proof Only	—	—	—
1877	A	—	—	—
1878	B	—	—	—
1879	B	—	—	—
1880	B	—	—	—
1881	B	—	—	—
1882	B	—	—	—
1883	B	—	—	—
1884	B	—	—	—
1885	B	—	—	—
1886	B	—	—	—
1887	B	—	—	—
1888	B	—	—	—
1889	B	—	—	—

Explanatory Notes: B indicates more than 12 appearances in Uncirculated grade at public auction without regard to repetitious offerings, 1972-mid 1988; AAAA = 0 appearances; AAA = 1-3 appearances; AA = 4-6 appearances; A = 7-12 appearances; a dash indicates none minted.

in 1878 somewhat larger quantities of coins were made, in anticipation of a public demand, but this never materialized, so from then through the end of the series mintages were low. An interest in speculating in $3 pieces arose in 1879, so $3 pieces from this year through the end of the series are more plentiful in Uncirculated grade than their low mintages would suggest.

As is true in other gold series, there are many sleepers among $3 pieces. Coins of the first year of issue, 1854, are occasionally seen in MS-60 or better grade. Two reasons account for this: First, the mintage quantity of this year was large, so more were made to begin with. Second, the novelty of the design prompted some to set them aside as souvenirs. Philadelphia Mint $3 pieces from 1855 through 1877 are all rare in MS-60 or better condition, except for the higher-mintage 1874. A few branch mint varieties were minted: 1854-D, 1854-O, 1855-S, 1856-S, 1857-S, and 1860-S, and all are extreme rarities in Mint State. Then there is the 1870-S, a unique piece; just one exists.

In terms of sleepers, studying the auction appearances of various coins in the series will prove instructive, as it will for other gold series. The current *Guide Book* lists an MS-60 1878 $3 piece for $4,500, and an 1865 of the same denomination is listed for $6,500. In my professional experience, the 1865 is at least one hundred times rarer! Spotting sleepers is a lot of fun, and there certainly is money to be made, so if the subject interests you, delve into it, and you will be surprised to learn how many undervalued coins lurk among the issues listed.

CHAPTER FIVE

Stellas

In 1879 and 1880 $4 gold patterns were made in two styles, the Flowing Hair motif designed by Charles E. Barber, and the Coiled Hair format designed by George T. Morgan. These were proposals for an international coinage, on the theory that pieces of this denomination closely approximated the value of certain gold issues circulating in Europe.

Production for circulation never came to pass. Pattern coins proved popular with collectors from the very time of issue, and there was a sufficient demand for them that the Philadelphia Mint struck several hundred additional 1879 Flowing Hair coins. The numbers produced are suggested in the *Guide Book*, and are simply an approximation. Probably something short of 600 of the 1879 Flowing Hair pieces were minted, and much smaller quantities were made of the 1879 Coiled Hair, the 1880 Flowing Hair, and the 1880 Coiled Hair. Today, each of these varieties is highly desired, and when pieces cross the auction block or are offered at private sale they inevitably meet with an enthusiastic reception.

1879-1880 $4 STELLA Flowing Hair Type

Designed by: Charles E. Barber
Issue dates: 1879-1880
Composition: 0.93 part gold, 0.07 parts copper and silver
Diameter: 22 mm
Weight: Varies, typically 108-109 grains
Edge: Reeded
Proof mintage: Under 600 including restrikes

1879-1880 $4 STELLA Coiled Hair Type

Designed by: George T. Morgan
Issue dates: 1879-1880
Composition: 0.93 part gold, 0.07 parts copper and silver
Diameter: 22 mm
Weight: Varies, typically 108-109 grains
Edge: Reeded
Proof mintage: Approximately 25

CHAPTER SIX

Half Eagles

The $5 gold piece, or half eagle, represents the first gold denomination issued by the Philadelphia Mint. The initial delivery of coins occurred on July 1, 1795. The Mint Act of April 2, 1792 provided for a gold half eagle and other gold coins, but certain Mint officials were not able to meet the high surety bond requirements to coin precious metals, so mintage did not occur until 1795.

In the early years, half eagles were the workhorse coins of American commerce. From 1795 through 1834, many more pieces of this denomination were made than of the other two gold issues, the quarter eagle and the eagle.

By 1834, the price of gold bullion had risen sufficiently on the international market that a profit could be made by converting minted coins to bullion. The result was that the vast majority of early half eagles went to the melting pot. Although tens of thousands of half eagles were made of certain issues in the 1820s, today the number of known specimens is enumerated in dozens, if not even fewer. Melting provides the explanation.

Half eagles of the 1795-1834 years are the "rarest of the rare" in American numismatics. All are elusive, and some are

HALF EAGLE: 1795-1798 Small Eagle Reverse

Designed by: Robert Scot
Issue dates: 1795-1798
Composition: 0.9167 part gold, 0.0833 part copper
Diameter: 25 mm
Weight: 135 grains
Edge: Reeded
Business strike mintage: 18,512
Proof mintage: None

HALF EAGLE: 1795-1807 Heraldic Eagle Reverse

Designed by: Robert Scot
Issue dates: 1795-1807
Composition: 0.9167 part gold, 0.0833 part copper
Diameter: 25 mm
Weight: 135 grains
Edge: Reeded
Business strike mintage: 316,867
Proof mintage: None

HALF EAGLE: 1807-1812 Capped Draped Bust to Left

Designed by: John Reich
Issue dates: 1807-1812
Composition: 0.9167 part gold, 0.0833 part copper
Diameter: 25 mm
Weight: 135 grains
Edge: Reeded
Business strike mintage: 399,013
Proof mintage: None

HALF EAGLE: 1813-1834 Capped Head to Left

Designed by: John Reich
Issue dates: 1813-1834
Composition: 0.9167 part gold, 0.0833 part copper
Diameter: 25 mm (1813-1829), 22.5 mm (1829-1834)
Weight: 135 grains
Edge: Reeded
Business strike mintage: 1,385,612
Proof mintage: Fewer than 150

major rarities. In the latter category are such issues as the 1798 with Small Eagle reverse, the 1797 with 16-star obverse and Heraldic Eagle reverse (unique, in the Smithsonian Institution), and most dates of the with motto (E PLURIBUS UNUM) style from 1819 through 1834.

The spotlight has fallen upon the 1822 half eagle, of which just three specimens are known. Two are in the Smithsonian Institution, and the third was catalogued by the present writer as part of the Eliasberg Collection of United States Gold Coins (October 1982), at which auction event it crossed the block at $687,500.

While some may aspire to assemble a date and variety collection of half eagles from 1795 through 1834, doing so requires a very generous budget combined with a great deal of patience. Over a period of years it should be possible to acquire all but a few varieties in this date span.

More popular is collecting them by major design types. A type set of early half eagles, while not exactly "affordable" in the popular sense, can be completed without a great deal of difficulty. Such a set consists of one each of the Capped Bust to Right style with Small Eagle reverse, dated from 1795 through 1798; the somewhat overlapping Capped Bust to Right obverse combined with the Heraldic Eagle reverse, 1795-1807; the Capped Draped Bust to Left style 1807-1812; the Capped Head to Left, large diameter, style 1813-1829; and the Capped Head to Left, smaller diameter, style 1829-1834.

Beginning on August 1, 1834, half eagles were made of reduced weight. After that point, the coins circulated and were free from melting and speculating considerations, for the intrinsic value was sufficiently below the face value that such was not profitable. The new coins are designated by collectors as the Classic Head style and are the work of William Kneass, Mint engraver. The same format was used on contemporary quarter eagles. Classic Head half eagles of the 1834-1838 years are readily available in lower grades, except for the 1838-C and 1838-D, which are scarce in any preservation. Philadelphia Mint

HALF EAGLE: 1834-1838 Classic Head

Designed by: William Kneass
Issue dates: 1834-1838
Composition: 0.8992 part gold, 0.1008 part copper
Diameter: 22.5 mm
Weight: 129 grains
Edge: Reeded
Business strike mintage: 2,113,612
Proof mintage: Fewer than 50

coins in AU or better grades are scarce, and pieces in MS-60 or finer preservation are decidedly rare.

In 1839 the Coronet or Braided Hair type made its appearance. The work of Christian Gobrecht, the style was employed continuously from then through 1908. Beginning in 1866 the motto IN GOD WE TRUST was added to the reverse.

Coronet half eagles minted from 1839 through the mid-1870s exist today in worn grades in approximate proportion to the mintage quantities. Those produced in large numbers are relatively common, while reduced mintage issues, such as those of the Charlotte and Dahlonega mints, are seldom seen. Uncirculated coins are a different breed of cat. Many are the so-called "common" issues which are easy enough to find in worn grades, but which are great rarities in Uncirculated grade. Indeed, some pieces are so rare that a span of years may elapse between offerings.

As is the case with quarter eagles, many issues are far rarer than the *Guide Book* values suggest. For example, the first year of issue, 1839, is posted at $2,000 in MS-60 grade. However, it is unlikely if as many as 10 examples exist in all of numismatics. I imagine that, if offered at auction, an MS-60 piece would bring *multiples* of the *Guide Book* price.

Beginning with pieces dated toward the end of the 1870s, half eagles are more plentiful in Uncirculated condition, and many issues toward the end of the Coronet series are actually common. For example, there will be no difficulty at all experienced in acquiring an MS-60 or better specimen of 1901-S, one of the highest mintage coins in the series.

There are many sleepers to be found among Coronet half eagles. Among issues from 1839 through the 1870s, these can be spotted by checking auction records, many of which have be enumerated in David Akers' study on the subject. This procedure will prove useful for later issues as well.

Among later pieces the 1904-S catalogues $400 in MS-60 grade in the current *Guide Book*, the same price as listed for the common 1901-S, and yet in MS-60 grade the 1904-S is prob-

HALF EAGLE: 1839-1866 Coronet

Designed by: Christian Gobrecht
Issue dates: 1839-1866
Composition: 0.900 part gold, 0.100 part copper
Diameter: 22.5 mm (1839-1840); 21.6 mm (1840-1866)
Weight: 129.0 grains
Edge: Reeded
Business strike mintage: 9,114,049
Proof mintage: 450 (estimated)

HALF EAGLE: 1866-1908 Coronet, With Motto

Designed by: Christian Gobrecht
Issue dates: 1866-1908
Composition: 0.900 part gold, 0.100 part copper
Diameter: 21.6 mm
Weight: 129.0 grains
Edge: Reeded
Business strike mintage: 51,503,654
Proof mintage: 2,938

ably at least *several hundred times rarer*. This does not mean that a 1904-S has the potential of being worth several hundred times the price of a 1901-S, for it doesn't. The reason is that relatively few people collect half eagles by date and mintmark sequence, so the greatest demand is for pieces as "types." The type collector does not care whether he has a 1901-S or 1904-S, and would not pay significantly more for a 1904-S, even though it is rarer. I suggest, however, that if you are collecting coins by design types, the adding of scarcer issues to your type set is a good idea, if you can find them for little or more than common prices. The appeal of owning something that is scarce or rare adds an extra dimension to whatever you own.

Among half eagles of the Coronet style, acquiring one of each of the two design types—the style without motto, minted from 1839 through 1866; and the style with IN GOD WE TRUST minted from 1866 through 1908—will present no difficulty. As indicated, obtaining an MS-60 example of a later issue such as 1901-S will be a snap. Among earlier issues, 1839 through 1866, EF-45 to AU-55 is a more reasonable goal, although occasional MS-60 coins do come on the market.

In 1908 the Indian Head half eagle made its appearance. The design counterpart to the quarter eagle, the piece was the work of Bela Lyon Pratt, a noted Boston sculptor. The designs and inscriptions are incuse or recessed in the surface, with the field or background being the highest point. From the aspect of grading, this presents unusual considerations, as even coin-to-coin contact in a mint bag soon resulted in pieces having a somewhat scuffed appearance. Using today's strict grading interpretations, even MS-60 examples of certain otherwise common issues are hard to find. Thus, a variety such as 1911-S, which was minted in large quantities, is common enough in lower grades, but in Uncirculated preservation is very difficult to find. In MS-63 grade many Indian Head half eagles are rare. In MS-65 or better grade, there are numerous extreme rarities. One of the first to point this out was Mike Brownlee, who mentioned to me about ten years ago that in MS-65 grade there were

HALF EAGLE: 1908-1929 Indian

Designed by: Bela Lyon Pratt
Issue dates: 1908-1929
Composition: 0.900 part gold, 0.100 part copper
Diameter: 21.6 mm
Weight: 129 grains
Edge: Reeded
Business strike mintage: 14,078,066
Proof mintage: 1,077

numerous varieties of Indian Head half eagles which everyone thought were "common," but when one actually looked for them, they were not to be found. As more coins are evaluated using today's conservative grading interpretations, expect the pricing structure of "common" half eagles, as we know it today, to be rearranged!

In the Indian Head half eagle series there are two well-known rarities, pieces which are scarce in *any* grade. The first is the 1909-O, which had the low mintage of just 34,200 pieces. The second is the 1929, the last coin in the series. A study of mintage figures shows that 662,000 examples of the 1929 were minted, one of the most generous productions in the entire series. However, unknown to the casual observer is the fact that most of these were stored in Treasury vaults, never released, and went to the melting pot around 1934. It is probably the case that only a couple of hundred pieces survive today.

Half Eagles

	Philadelphia	Carson City	Charlotte
1838	B	—	AAA
1839	A	—	AAA
1840	A	—	AAA
1841	AAA	—	A
1842 Small Letters	AAAA	—	—
1842 Large Letters	AAAA	—	—
1842 Small Date	—	—	AAA
1842 Large Date	—	—	AA
1843 Small Letters	—	—	AAA
1843 Large Letters	B	—	—
1844	B	—	AA
1845	B	—	—
1846	B	—	AAA
1847	B	—	AAA
1848	B	—	AAA
1849	AA	—	A
1850	AAA	—	AAA
1851	B	—	AAAA
1852	B	—	AA
1853	B	—	A
1854	A	—	AAA
1855	B	—	AA
1856	B	—	AAA
1857	B	—	A
1858	A	—	A
1859	AA	—	A
1860	AAA	—	A
1861	B	—	AAA
1862	AAAA	—	—
1863	AAA	—	—
1864	AAA	—	—
1865	AAAA	—	—
1866 No Motto	—	—	—
1866 Motto	AAA	—	—
1867	AAAA	—	—
1868	AAA	—	—
1869	AAAA	—	—
1870	AAAA	AAAA	—
1871	AAAA	AAA	—
1872	AA	AAAA	—
1873 Closed 3	AAA	AAAA	—
1873 Open 3	A	—	—
1874	AAAA	AAA	—
1875	AAAA	AAAA	—
1876	AAA	AAA	—
1877	AAA	AAAA	—
1878	B	AAAA	—
1879	B	AAA	—
1880	B	AA	—

Explanatory Notes: B indicates more than 12 appearances in Uncirculated grade at public auction without regard to repetitious offerings, 1972-mid 1988; AAAA = 0 appearances; AAA = 1-3 appearances; AA = 4-6 appearances; A = 7-12 appearances; a dash indicates none minted.

1838-1880

Dahlonega	Denver	New Orleans	San Francisco
B	—	—	—
AAA	—	—	—
AAA	—	A	—
A	—	—	—
—	—	—	—
—	—	—	—
A	—	AAAA	—
AAAA	—	—	—
—	—	AA	—
AA	—	AAA	—
A	—	B	—
B	—	AAA	—
AA	—	AAAA	—
A	—	AAAA	—
AAAA	—	—	—
AAA	—	—	—
AAAA	—	—	—
AAA	—	AAAA	—
AA	—	—	—
B	—	—	—
B	—	AA	AAAA
AA	—	AAAA	AA
AAA	—	AAAA	AAA
AA	—	AAAA	AAA
AAA	—	—	AAAA
AA	—	—	AAA
A	—	—	AAA
A	—	—	AAAA
—	—	—	AAAA
—	—	—	AAAA
—	—	—	AAA
—	—	—	AAAA
—	—	—	AAAA
—	—	—	AAAA
—	—	—	AAAA
—	—	—	AAA
—	—	—	AAAA
—	—	—	AAAA
—	—	—	AAA
—	—	—	AAA
—	—	—	AAAA
—	—	—	—
—	—	—	AAAA
—	—	—	AAAA
—	—	—	AAA
—	—	—	AAA
—	—	—	AA
—	—	—	B
—	—	—	B

Explanatory Notes: B indicates more than 12 appearances in Uncirculated grade at public auction without regard to repetitious offerings, 1972-mid 1988; AAAA = 0 appearances; AAA = 1-3 appearances; AA = 4-6 appearances; A = 7-12 appearances; a dash indicates none minted.

Half Eagles

	Philadelphia	Carson City	Charlotte
1881	B	AA	—
1882	B	A	—
1883	B	AA	—
1884	A	AAA	—
1885	B	—	—
1886	B	—	—
1887	Proof Only	—	—
1888	A	—	—
1889	B	—	—
1890	AA	B	—
1891	B	B	—
1892	B	B	—
1893	B	B	—
1894	B	—	—
1895	B	—	—
1896	B	—	—
1897	B	—	—
1898	B	—	—
1899	B	—	—
1900	B		
1901	B	—	—
1902	B	—	—
1903	B	—	—
1904	B	—	—
1905	B	—	—
1906	B	—	—
1907	B	—	—
1908	B	—	—
1909	B	—	—
1910	B	—	—
1911	B	—	—
1912	B	—	—
1913	B	—	—
1914	B	—	—
1915	B	—	—
1916	—	—	—
1917	—	—	—
1918	—	—	—
1919	—	—	—
1920	—	—	—
1921	—	—	—
1922	—	—	—
1923	—	—	—
1924	—	—	—
1925	—	—	—
1926	—	—	—
1927	—	—	—
1928	—	—	—
1929	B	—	—

Explanatory Notes: B indicates more than 12 appearances in Uncirculated grade at public auction without regard to repetitious offerings, 1972-mid 1988; AAAA = 0 appearances; AAA = 1-3 appearances; AA = 4-6 appearances; A = 7-12 appearances; a dash indicates none minted.

1881-1929

Dahlonega	Denver	New Orleans	San Francisco
—	—	—	B
—	—	—	B
—	—	—	B
—	—	—	B
—	—	—	B
—	—	—	B
—	—	—	B
—	—	—	AAA
—	—	—	—
—	—	—	—
—	—	—	—
—	—	AA	B
—	—	B	B
—	—	B	A
—	—	—	AAA
—	—	—	A
—	—	—	A
—	—	—	B
—	—	—	B
—	—	—	B
—	—	—	B
—	—	—	B
—	—	—	B
—	—	—	B
—	—	—	B
—	B	—	B
—	B	—	—
—	B	—	B
—	B	B	B
—	B	—	B
—	B	—	B
—	—	—	B
—	—	—	B
—	B	—	B
—	—	—	B
—	—	—	B
—	—	—	—
—	—	—	—
—	—	—	—
—	—	—	—
—	—	—	—
—	—	—	—
—	—	—	—
—	—	—	—
—	—	—	—
—	—	—	—

Explanatory Notes: B indicates more than 12 appearances in Uncirculated grade at public auction without regard to repetitious offerings, 1972-mid 1988; AAAA = 0 appearances; AAA = 1-3 appearances; AA = 4-6 appearances; A = 7-12 appearances; a dash indicates none minted.

CHAPTER SEVEN

Eagles

Eagles, or $10 pieces, were first minted in 1795. Production was accomplished from that time through the year 1804, except that no examples were struck with the date 1802. In this range all pieces are scarce, although none is impossibly rare.

The collector of gold coins by design types is confronted with just two varieties. The first is the Capped Bust to Right style with Small Eagle reverse, for which coins dated 1795, 1796, and 1797 exist; and the second is the Capped Bust to Right, Heraldic Eagle reverse style, for which coins dated from 1797 through 1804 were made.

Coinage of the $10 denomination was suspended in 1804. In 1838 it was resumed, at which time the Coronet or Braided Hair type, by Christian Gobrecht, was used. Coins of this style were minted continuously through 1907. Coronet eagles are divided into two major types: those minted from 1838 through 1866, without motto on the reverse, and those minted from 1866 through 1907 with IN GOD WE TRUST above the eagle.

The availability situation of eagles approximates that of half eagles. Issues from 1838 through the late 1870s are available in worn grades in approximate proportion to their mintages.

EAGLE: 1795-1797 Small Eagle Reverse

Designed by: Robert Scot
Issue dates: 1795-1797
Composition: 0.9167 part gold, 0.0833 part copper
Diameter: 33 mm
Weight: 270 grains
Edge: Reeded
Business strike mintage: 13,344
Proof mintage: None

EAGLE: 1797-1804 Heraldic Eagle Reverse

Designed by: Robert Scot
Issue dates: 1797-1804
Composition: 0.9167 part gold, 0.0833 part copper
Diameter: 33 mm
Weight: 270 grains
Edge: Reeded
Business strike mintage: 119,248
Proof mintage: None

EAGLE: 1838-1866 Coronet

Designed by: Christian Gobrecht
Issue dates: 1838-1866
Composition: 0.900 part gold, 0.100 part copper
Diameter: 27 mm
Weight: 258 grains
Edge: Reeded
Business strike mintage: 5,292,499
Proof mintage: 400 (estimated)

EAGLE: 1866-1907 Coronet, With Motto

Designed by: Christian Gobrecht
Issue dates: 1866-1907
Composition: 0.900 part gold, 0.100 part copper
Diameter: 27 mm
Weight: 258 grains
Edge: Reeded
Business strike mintage: 37,391,767
Proof mintage: 2,327

MS-60 coins are rare for all issues, and for some issues are so rare that a span of many years may elapse between offerings. Again, there are numerous sleepers and unidentified rarities among the *Guide Book* listings, coins which list for a few thousand dollars in MS-60 grade, but for which no examples have crossed the auction block for a decade or more!

After the late 1870s, gold coins were hoarded in quantities by overseas banks. When the United States suspended the paying out of gold coins in 1933, and mandated that American citizens turn their coins in, foreign banks held onto their supplies. In recent decades, as worldwide interest in collecting gold coins has increased, bank hoards have been searched, and many Uncirculated pieces dating back to the 1880s have come to light. However, in the $10 series most such bank hoard coins for dates prior to 1900 show extensive bag marking, as no thought was given to preserving them carefully. Eagles of the 1900-1907 years are occasionally seen in MS-63 to MS-65 grades and are more available than their earlier counterparts.

Although $10 pieces of the 1838-1907 era are quite interesting, for some reason they have never caught on in a big way with collectors. While the double eagle, the larger cousin of the $10 piece, has always attracted a wide following, specialists who desire one of each date and mintmark variety of $10 pieces have been far fewer in number. This is beneficial for anyone aspiring to collect the series, for many prime rarities are available for nominal cost. This is particularly true among issues prior to the 1870s. There are numerous issues for which EF and AU coins are seldom seen in the marketplace, and yet the *Guide Book* value is apt to be less than $1,000 each.

In 1907 Augustus Saint-Gaudens' Indian design appeared. This piece was at once popular with numismatists and was favorably reviewed in various collectors' publications. Coinage of the Indian motif was continuous through 1916, although not accomplished at each of the branch mints. After 1916, the mintage was sporadic and included just 1920-S, 1926, 1930-S, 1932, and 1933.

EAGLE: 1907-1908 Indian, No Motto

Designed by: Augustus Saint-Gaudens
Issue dates: 1907-1908
Composition: 0.900 part gold, 0.100 part copper
Diameter: 27 mm
Weight: 258 grains
Edge: 46 raised stars
Business strike mintage: 483,448
Proof mintage: None of regular issue

EAGLE: 1908-1933 Indian, With Motto

Designed by: Augustus Saint-Gaudens
Issue dates: 1908-1933
Composition: 0.900 part gold, 0.100 part copper
Diameter: 27 mm
Weight: 258 grains
Edge: 46 stars 1908-1911; 48 stars 1912-1933
Business strike mintage: 14,385,139
Proof mintage: 768

The design of the Indian $10 is such that coins given a small amount of handling, including jostling against other coins in a mint bag, show marks very readily. Hence, according to today's strict grading interpretations, relatively few examples exist for the grades of MS-63 or above. Exceptions to this rule are two issues: 1926 and 1932, which came to light in quantity in foreign bank hoards; these coins are readily available. It is probably correct to say that so far as MS-63 coins are concerned, there are at least three or four times as many 1926 and 1932 issues extant than there are for all other Indian varieties combined!

Among issues of the 1907-1916 years, there are many sleepers in higher grades. Even MS-60 examples are quite difficult to find of just about every issue, and the appearance of MS-63 or MS-65 coins is apt to excite even the most seasoned gold specialist. As is the case with half eagles of this era, the pricing structure of some of the "common" coins will be rearranged once these issues are studied in detail.

Among Indian eagles there are a number of rarities, including the with-periods varieties of 1907, the 1920-S, the 1930-S, and the 1933. Mintage figures cannot be correlated to availability in many instances. Thus, 1920-S, with a mintage of 126,500, is a great rarity in any condition, while 1915-S, with a mintage of 59,000, is easily available in lower grades (but is rare in Mint State, however). It is undoubtedly the case that nearly all of the 1920-S pieces were stored by the Treasury Department and then melted circa 1934. The same thing happened with the issues of 1930-S and 1933.

While a number of collectors have endeavored to assemble a set of Indian eagles by date and mint variety, the most popular way to acquire them is by type. Discounting the limited-mintage varieties of 1907 with periods before and after E PLURIBUS UNUM, there are just two main design types in the series: the 1907-1908 style without motto, and the 1908-1933 type with IN GOD WE TRUST.

Eagles

	Philadelphia	Carson City	Denver
1838	A	—	—
1839 Type of '38	A	—	—
1839 Type of '40	AAA	—	—
1840	A	—	—
1841	AAA	—	—
1842 Small Date	AAA	—	—
1842 Large Date	AAAA	—	—
1843	AAAA	—	—
1844	AAAA	—	—
1845	AAA	—	—
1846	AAAA	—	—
1847	B	—	—
1848	A	—	—
1849	A	—	—
1850	A	—	—
1851	AA	—	—
1852	B	—	—
1853	B	—	—
1854	AA	—	—
1855	B	—	—
1856	A	—	—
1857	AAA	—	—
1858	AAA	—	—
1859	AAA	—	—
1860	AA	—	—
1861	A	—	—
1862	AAA	—	—
1863	AAAA	—	—
1864	AAAA	—	—
1865	AAA	—	—
1866 No Motto	—	—	—
1866 Motto	AAAA	—	—
1867	AAAA	—	—
1868	AAAA	—	—
1869	AAA	—	—
1870	AAA	AAAA	—
1871	AAAA	AAAA	—
1872	AAA	AAAA	—
1873	AAAA	AAAA	—
1874	A	AAA	—
1875	AAAA	AAAA	—
1876	AAAA	AAAA	—
1877	AAA	AAA	—
1878	B	AAAA	—
1879	B	AAAA	—
1880	B	AA	—
1881	B	B	—
1882	B	A	—
1883	B	A	—
1884	A	AAAA	—

Explanatory Notes: B indicates more than 12 appearances in Uncirculated grade at public auction without regard to repetitious offerings, 1972-mid 1988; AAAA = 0 appearances; AAA = 1-3 appearances; AA = 4-6 appearances; A = 7-12 appearances; a dash indicates none minted.

1838-1884

	New Orleans	San Francisco
1838	—	—
1839 Type of '38	—	—
1839 Type of '40	—	—
1840	—	—
1841	AAAA	—
1842 Small Date	—	—
1842 Large Date	A	—
1843	AA	—
1844	AAA	—
1845	AA	—
1846	AAA	—
1847	B	—
1848	AAAA	—
1849	AAA	—
1850	AAA	—
1851	AA	—
1852	AAAA	—
1853	AAAA	—
1854	AAAA	AAA
1855	AAA	AAA
1856	AAAA	AA
1857	AAAA	AAAA
1858	A	AAAA
1859	AAAA	AAAA
1860	A	AAAA
1861	—	AAAA
1862	—	AAAA
1863	—	AAAA
1864	—	AAAA
1865	—	AAAA
1866 No Motto	—	AAAA
1866 Motto	—	AAAA
1867	—	AAAA
1868	—	AAAA
1869	—	AAA
1870	—	AAAA
1871	—	AAAA
1872	—	AAA
1873	—	AAA
1874	—	AAAA
1875	—	—
1876	—	AAA
1877	—	AAAA
1878	—	AAAA
1879	AAA	A
1880	AA	B
1881	AAAA	B
1882	AA	B
1883	AAAA	A
1884	—	A

Explanatory Notes: B indicates more than 12 appearances in Uncirculated grade at public auction without regard to repetitious offerings, 1972-mid 1988; AAAA = 0 appearances; AAA = 1-3 appearances; AA = 4-6 appearances; A = 7-12 appearances; a dash indicates none minted.

Eagles

	Philadelphia	Carson City	Denver
1885	B	—	—
1886	B	—	—
1887	AA	—	—
1888	AA	—	—
1889	B	—	—
1890	B	B	—
1891	B	B	—
1892	B	B	—
1893	B	AA	—
1894	B	—	—
1895	B	—	—
1896	B	—	—
1897	B	—	—
1898	B	—	—
1899	B	—	—
1900	B	—	—
1901	B	—	—
1902	B	—	—
1903	B	—	—
1904	B	—	—
1905	B	—	—
1906	B	—	B
1907	B	—	B
1908	B	—	B
1909	B	—	B
1910	B	—	B
1911	B	—	B
1912	B	—	—
1913	B	—	—
1914	B	—	B
1915	B	—	—
1916	—	—	—
1917	—	—	—
1918	—	—	—
1919	—	—	—
1920	—	—	—
1921	—	—	—
1922	—	—	—
1923	—	—	—
1924	—	—	—
1925	—	—	—
1926	B	—	—
1927	—	—	—
1928	—	—	—
1929	—	—	—
1930	—	—	—
1931	—	—	—
1932	B	—	—
1933	B	—	—

Explanatory Notes: B indicates more than 12 appearances in Uncirculated grade at public auction without regard to repetitious offerings, 1972-mid 1988; AAAA = 0 appearances; AAA = 1-3 appearances; AA = 4-6 appearances; A = 7-12 appearances; a dash indicates none minted.

1885-1933

	New Orleans	San Francisco
1885	—	B
1886	—	B
1887	—	B
1888	B	B
1889	—	B
1890	—	—
1891	—	—
1892	B	B
1893	B	B
1894	B	AAA
1895	B	AAA
1896	—	AAA
1897	B	B
1898	—	B
1899	B	B
1900	—	A
1901	B	B
1902	—	B
1903	B	B
1904	B	—
1905	—	B
1906	B	B
1907	—	B
1908	—	B
1909	—	B
1910	—	B
1911	—	B
1912	—	B
1913	—	B
1914	—	B
1915	—	B
1916	—	B
1917	—	—
1918	—	—
1919	—	—
1920	—	B
1921	—	—
1922	—	—
1923	—	—
1924	—	—
1925	—	—
1926	—	—
1927	—	—
1928	—	—
1929	—	—
1930	—	B
1931	—	—
1932	—	—
1933	—	—

Explanatory Notes: B indicates more than 12 appearances in Uncirculated grade at public auction without regard to repetitious offerings, 1972-mid 1988; AAAA = 0 appearances; AAA = 1-3 appearances; AA = 4-6 appearances; A = 7-12 appearances; a dash indicates none minted.

CHAPTER EIGHT

Double Eagles

The large, heavy, and impressive double eagle, or $20 gold piece, first minted for circulation in 1850, has always been a popular denomination with numismatists. Even though "the price of admission" is apt to be the best part of $1,000 even for a common issue, because of its gold content of nearly an ounce, and the numismatic premium above that, still these coins have attracted a large following over the years. Even though collecting by date and mintmark has been popular, relatively speaking, most who acquire double eagles purchase them as part of a type set. The series neatly divides itself into several types, each of which is affordable.

The Liberty Head type, by James Longacre, made its appearance in 1850 and was continued in production through 1907. Three variations were made: the first, minted from 1850 through 1866, has no motto and has the denomination expressed as TWENTY D. The second, minted from 1866 through 1876, is similar except that IN GOD WE TRUST has been added above the eagle. The third, minted from 1877 to 1907, retains the motto above the eagle but has the denomination expressed differently, as TWENTY DOLLARS.

DOUBLE EAGLES: 1849-1866 Coronet

Designed by: James Barton Longacre
Issue dates: 1849 (pattern); 1850-1866
Composition: 0.900 part gold, 0.100 part copper
Diameter: 34 mm
Weight: 516 grains
Edge: Reeded
Business strike mintage: 23,526,676
Proof mintage: 375 (estimated)

$20: 1866-1876 Coronet, With Motto TWENTY D.

Designed by: James Barton Longacre
Issue dates: 1866-1876
Composition: 0.900 part gold, 0.100 part copper
Diameter: 30 mm
Weight: 516 grains
Edge: Reeded
Business strike mintage: 16,160,758
Proof mintage: 335

DOUBLE EAGLE: 1877-1907 Coronet, 20 DOLLARS

Designed by: James Barton Longacre
Issue dates: 1877-1907
Composition: 0.900 part gold, 0.100 part copper
Diameter: 30 mm
Weight: 516 grains
Edge: Reeded
Business strike mintage: 64,137,477
Proof mintage: 2,426

In general, double eagles of the 19th century are available in worn grades in proportion to their original mintages. In Uncirculated preservation the story is different and follows the theme of $5 and $10 pieces. Coins dated prior to the mid-1870s are exceedingly scarce in MS-60 preservation, rarer yet in MS-63 grade, and are extreme rarities in MS-65 or better. From the late 1870s through 1907, Uncirculated pieces are more readily available, although those dated before 1890 are apt to be extensively bag marked. In terms of Uncirculated pieces, the most common Liberty Head double eagle is the 1904, of which large overseas hoards have been distributed. After the 1904, there are several varieties of its era which can be obtained with some searching, although certain issues, even those with high mintages, are apt to be elusive. A study of auction and price list appearances will reveal numerous sleepers.

The Liberty Head series is studded with a number of prime rarities, the most famous of which is the 1861 Philadelphia Mint issue with the Paquet Reverse (with tall letters). Just two of these are known. Beyond this, there are such rarities as the 1883, 1884, and 1887, made only with Proof finish, the rare 1854-O and 1856-O New Orleans issues, the very rare 1870-CC, and a handful of other varieties which are seldom seen.

In 1907 the Saint-Gaudens High Relief double eagle with Roman numeral date MCMVII appeared and created a sensation. From day one these were popular with collectors and the public alike. Today, the issue remains a classic and is high on the "most wanted list" of many collectors. Time and time again, surveys have been made to determine America's most beautiful coin made for circulation, and time and time again the MCMVII has won the honors. Indeed, in 1986 when the United States government decided to make bullion-type gold coins, they could find no motif better than Saint-Gaudens' work of 1907, so they resurrected it for further use.

Among double eagles of the 1907-1933 Saint-Gaudens style, there are a number of scarcities and rarities. The MCMVII issue, made only during the first year, is not a great rarity, but

DOUBLE EAGLE: MCMVII (1907) High Relief

Designed by: Augustus Saint-Gaudens
Issue date: 1907
Composition: 0.900 part gold, 0.100 part copper
Diameter: 34 mm
Weight: 516 grains
Edge: Lettered E PLURIBUS UNUM with stars interspersing
Business strike mintage: 11,250
Proof mintage: Fewer than 25

the demand is so great for it that it is among the more expensive issues in the series. Other issues from 1907 through 1933 have the date in so-called Arabic numerals. Among these, rarities in *any* grade include 1920-S, 1921, 1927-D (in particular, fewer than 10 are in collectors' hands), 1927-S, 1929, 1930-S, 1931, 1931-D, and 1932. Although 445,500 double eagles dated 1933 were minted, the government takes the stand that none was officially placed in circulation. A few have appeared on the market from time to time over the years and have been seized as being illegally held, a position which seems, at least to the present writer, to be open to challenge—but arguing with the government may be futile! In February and early March 1933 it was theoretically possible to have obtained a 1933 double eagle from the government by paying face value for it.

For all practical purposes, a "complete" set of Saint-Gaudens double eagles contains varieties from 1907 through 1932, excluding the 1933.

Among earlier issues in the series, those from 1907 through 1916, worn examples exist in approximate relationship to their original mintages. Uncirculated coins are a different question entirely. There are numerous sleepers awaiting the alert student of the series. Take, for example, the two issues of 1908 from the Philadelphia Mint. There were 4,271,551 examples made of the style without motto, but only 156,359 made with IN GOD WE TRUST on the reverse. And yet, each catalogues at just $850 in MS-60 grade. Of the 1908 Without Motto style, bank hoards have been dispersed, so this issue stands today as the most common of its era so far as MS-63 to MS-65 coins are concerned. Not so with the 1908 With Motto style. This issue is very rare, and in MS-63 to MS-65 grade is at least 100 times rarer than its earlier counterpart! So, here is a sleeper for anyone who cares to search for one.

In the grades of MS-63 to MS-65 there are numerous other early rarities, including all with-motto issues from 1908 through 1916-S inclusive. Particularly hard to find are branch mint issues. You might be skeptical of this statement at first glance,

DOUBLE EAGLE: 1907-1908 No Motto

Designed by: Augustus Saint-Gaudens
Issue dates: 1907-1908
Composition: 0.900 part gold, 0.100 part copper
Diameter: 34 mm
Weight: 516 grains
Edge: Lettered E PLURIBUS UNUM
Business strike mintage: 5,294,968
Proof mintage: Fewer than 5

DOUBLE EAGLE: 1908-1933 With Motto

Designed by: Augustus Saint-Gaudens
Issue dates: 1908-1933
Composition: 0.900 part gold, 0.100 part copper
Diameter: 34 mm
Weight: 516 grains
Edge: Lettered E PLURIBUS UNUM
Business strike mintage: 64,981,428
Proof mintage: 687

for the *Guide Book* does not reflect the scarcity, but such is really the case, and if you are able to buy some of these pieces you should do very well financially. Just about any one of the with-motto issues from 1908 through 1916 is several hundred times rarer than the previously-mentioned 1908 Without Motto, and yet the 1908 Without Motto catalogues for more than many of the later issues do!

Double eagles from 1920 through 1932, although many are scarce, exist in higher average grades, for they circulated very little. In general, the most readily available pieces are Philadelphia Mint issues from 1924 through 1928 inclusive. Branch mint issues from 1924 onward are rare in all instances.

While the collector by date and mintmark certainly has challenges awaiting him in the completion of a 1907-1932 collection, particularly with the landmark 1927-D, the type set collector will have an easy time of it. A type set of Saint-Gaudens pieces can consist of two coins, or three coins, as you prefer. If you add the MCMVII High Relief issue, the set will contain three pieces. Otherwise it will contain just two: an example of the 1907-1908 style without-motto, of which the much-discussed 1908 is relatively available in Mint State; and the 1908-1932 style with-motto, of which you will have no difficulty in obtaining as Mint State specimen of one of the Philadelphia Mint years circa 1924-1928.

Double Eagles

	Philadelphia	Carson City	Denver
1849	Unique	—	—
1850	B	—	—
1851	B	—	—
1852	B	—	—
1853	B	—	—
1854	B	—	—
1855	B	—	—
1856	B	—	—
1857	B	—	—
1858	B	—	—
1859	AAA	—	—
1860	B	—	—
1861	B	—	—
1861 Paquet	AAAA	—	—
1862	AAA	—	—
1863	AAA	—	—
1864	AA	—	—
1865	B	—	—
1866 No Motto			—
1866 Motto	B	—	—
1867	B	—	—
1868	AA	—	—
1869	A	—	—
1870	AA	AAAA	—
1871	AA	AAA	—
1872	B	AAA	—
1873 Closed 3	AAA	AAA	—
1873 Open 3	B	—	—
1874	B	A	—
1875	B	B	—
1876	B	B	—
1877	B	B	—
1878	B	AA	—
1879	B	AA	—
1880	A	—	—
1881	AAAA	—	—
1882	AAA	B	—
1883	Proof only	B	—
1884	Proof only	B	—
1885	A	B	—
1886	AAA	—	—
1887	Proof only	—	—
1888	B	—	—
1889	B	B	—

Explanatory Notes: B indicates more than 12 appearances in Uncirculated grade at public auction without regard to repetitious offerings, 1972-mid 1988; AAAA = 0 appearances; AAA = 1-3 appearances; AA = 4-6 appearances; A = 7-12 appearances; a dash indicates none minted.

1849-1889

	New Orleans	San Francisco
1849	—	—
1850	AAA	—
1851	A	—
1852	A	—
1853	AA	—
1854	AAA	B
1855	AAA	B
1856	AAAA	B
1857	AAA	B
1858	AA	A
1859	AAA	A
1860	AAAA	A
1861	AAAA	A
1861 Paquet	—	AAAA
1862	—	AA
1863	—	B
1864	—	AAA
1865	—	A
1866 No Motto	—	AAAA
1866 Motto	—	AA
1867	—	A
1868	—	A
1869	—	B
1870	—	B
1871	—	B
1872	—	B
1873 Closed 3	—	B
1873 Open 3	—	B
1874	—	B
1875	—	B
1876	—	B
1877	—	B
1878	—	B
1879	AA	B
1880	—	A
1881	—	B
1882	—	B
1883	—	B
1884	—	B
1885	—	B
1886	—	—
1887	—	B
1888	—	B
1889	—	B

Explanatory Notes: B indicates more than 12 appearances in Uncirculated grade at public auction without regard to repetitious offerings, 1972-mid 1988; AAAA = 0 appearances; AAA = 1-3 appearances; AA = 4-6 appearances; A = 7-12 appearances; a dash indicates none minted.

Double Eagles

	Philadelphia	Carson City	Denver
1890	B	B	—
1891	AA	A	—
1892	B	B	—
1893	B	B	—
1894	B	—	—
1895	B	—	—
1896	B	—	—
1897	B	—	—
1898	B	—	—
1899	B	—	—
1900	B	—	—
1901	B	—	—
1902	B	—	—
1903	B	—	—
1904	B	—	—
1905	B	—	—
1906	B	—	B
1907	B	—	B
1908	B	—	B
1909	B	—	B
1910	B	—	B
1911	B	—	B
1912	B	—	—
1913	B	—	B
1914	B	—	B
1915	B	—	—
1916	—	—	—
1917	—	—	—
1918	—	—	—
1919	—	—	—
1920	B	—	—
1921	B	—	—
1922	B	—	—
1923	B	—	B
1924	B	—	B
1925	B	—	B
1926	B	—	B
1927	B	—	AA
1928	B	—	—
1929	B	—	—
1930	—	—	—
1931	B	—	B
1932	B	—	—
1933	None placed in circulation	—	—

Explanatory Notes: B indicates more than 12 appearances in Uncirculated grade at public auction without regard to repetitious offerings, 1972-mid 1988; AAAA = 0 appearances; AAA = 1-3 appearances; AA = 4-6 appearances; A = 7-12 appearances; a dash indicates none minted.

1890-1933

	New Orleans	San Francisco
1890	—	B
1891	—	B
1892	—	B
1893	—	B
1894	—	B
1895	—	B
1896	—	B
1897	—	B
1898	—	B
1899	—	B
1900	—	B
1901	—	B
1902	—	B
1903	—	B
1904	—	B
1905	—	B
1906	—	B
1907	—	B
1908	—	B
1909	—	B
1910	—	B
1911	—	B
1912	—	—
1913	—	B
1914	—	B
1915	—	B
1916	—	B
1917	—	—
1918	—	—
1919	—	—
1920	—	B
1921	—	—
1922	—	B
1923	—	—
1924	—	B
1925	—	B
1926	—	B
1927	—	B
1928	—	—
1929	—	—
1930	—	B
1931	—	—
1932	—	—
1933	—	—

Explanatory Notes: B indicates more than 12 appearances in Uncirculated grade at public auction without regard to repetitious offerings, 1972-mid 1988; AAAA = 0 appearances; AAA = 1-3 appearances; AA = 4-6 appearances; A = 7-12 appearances; a dash indicates none minted.

CHAPTER NINE

Summary

The field of United States gold coins of the years from 1795 to 1933 is a rich and rewarding one for the astute buyer. Particularly among coins dated prior to the 1880s, there are numerous sleepers in just about every denomination from gold dollars through double eagles. From the standpoint of unrecognized rarities, the most fertile field is among higher grade specimens of issues 1834 and later, but before about 1878. *Guide Book* values do not reflect the rarity of many pieces, so one must go beyond this and study auction appearances and sale catalogue listings. The specific varieties listed in this book furnish many potentially profitable possibilities. Those who take the time to read this book and to study the market will find that in many instances a coin, if purchased at catalogue value, may be instantly worth *multiples* of that sum—certainly providing justification for whatever enjoyable effort might be expended in learning about such varieties!

Gold coins afford beautiful numismatic reminders of the days of long ago when a dollar was worth a dollar—and coins were struck in gold, the most famous and desired of all metals.

BIBLIOGRAPHY

Bibliography

Akers, David W., *United States Gold Coins: An Analysis of Auction Records.* (6 vols.) Paramount Publications, Englewood, Ohio, 1975-1982.

Akers, David W., *Handbook of 20th-Century United States Gold Coins.* Bowers and Merena Galleries, Wolfeboro, New Hampshire, 1988

Breen, Walter H., "Major Varieties of U.S. Gold Coins," Monographs (7 parts). Hewitt, Chicago, 1964-1966.

Bowers, Q. David, *United States Gold Coins: An Illustrated History.* Bowers and Merena Galleries, Wolfeboro, New Hampshire, 1984 (1982).

Krause Publications, *Auction Prices Realized: U.S. Coins.* (7 vols.) Iola, Wisconsin, 1982-1988.

Pollock, Andrew W. III, "Numismatic Register: U.S. Gold Coins 1838-1907." Privately published, 1988 (1985).

Rome's Reports, *Prices Realized for U.S. Coins.* (6 vols.) New York, 1979-1981.

Taxay, Don, *The Comprehensive Catalogue and Encyclopedia of United States Coins.* Scott Publishing Co., New York, 1975 (1970).

Yeoman, R.S., *A Guide Book of United States Coins.* Whitman Publishing Co., Racine, Wisconsin, 1987 (41st Rev. ed.)

Various individual auction sale catalogues from Auctions by Bowers and Merena, Inc., Heritage, Mid American, Pacific Coast, Paramount, Rarcoa, Superior Galleries, Stack's and other firms.

INDEX

Index

A
Akers, David, 14, 15, 18, 35, 52, 53, 76
Auction Prices Realized, 19

B
Barber, Charles E., 65, 66
Bell Collection, 52
Bowers, Q. David, 11, 15, 18
Bowers and Merena Galleries, 15, 19
Breen, Walter, 17
Brownlee, Mike, 79

C
California Gold Rush, 23
Carson City Mint, 28, 82, 84, 96, 98, 112, 114
Charlotte Mint, 25, 26, 33, 35, 41, 54, 56, 76, 82, 84
Civil War, 27, 33, 38, 59
"closed wreath," 33
Coin Dealer Newsletter, The, 15
Confederate notes, 27, 28
Confederate States of America, 27
Continental Currency, 24

D
Dahlonega Mint, 25, 26, 33, 35, 41, 54, 56, 61, 76, 83, 85
Denver Mint, 28, 55, 57, 83, 85, 96, 98, 112, 114

E
Eliasberg, Louis, 14
Eliasberg Collection, 14, 15, 25, 74
Encyclopedia of United States Coins, 18

F
Federal Reserve System, 29

G
Gobrecht, Christian, 49, 50, 76, 77, 78, 87, 90, 91
Gold Rush, 26
Gold Reserve Act, The, 30
"gold standard," 28, 30
Great Depression, 29
"greenbacks," 27
Guide Book of United States Coins, A, 14, 24, 25, 33, 38, 40, 43, 50, 52, 53, 62, 65, 76, 92, 110, 117

H
Handbook of 20th Century Gold Coins, A, 18

K
Kern Collection, 52
Kneass, William, 48, 50, 74, 75
Kosoff, Abe, 14
Krause Publications, 19

L

Longacre, James B., 33, 34, 36, 37, 59, 60, 101, 102, 103, 104

M

Melish, Thomas G. Collection, 13, 14
Mint Act of April 2, 1792, 69
Morgan, George T., 65, 67

N

New Netherlands Coin Company, 14
New Orleans Mint, 26, 33, 35, 41, 55, 57, 61, 83, 85, 97, 99, 113, 115
Norweb Collection, 13, 14
Norweb, Honorable and Mrs. R. Henry, 15
Numismatic Register, 19

P

Paquet Reverse, 105
Philadelphia Mint, 23, 25, 27, 33, 35, 38, 40, 41, 54, 56, 61, 62, 65, 69, 74, 82, 84, 96, 98, 105, 107, 110, 112, 114
Pollock, Andrew W. III, 19
Pratt, Bela Lyon, 50, 51, 79, 80
Pratt, coinages, 18

R

Reich, John, 46, 47, 72, 73
Rome's Reports, 19
Roosevelt, President Franklin D., 29

S

Saint-Gaudens, Augustus, 9, 18, 92, 93, 94, 105, 106, 107, 108, 109, 110
San Francisco Mint, 28, 38, 41, 55, 57, 61, 83, 85, 97, 99, 113, 115
Scot, Robert, 9, 44, 45, 70, 71, 88, 89
Smithsonian Institution, 74
Sutter's Mill, 26

T

Taxay, Don, 18
Treasury Department, 95

U

U.S. Gold Coins: An Illustrated History, 15

W

"wildcat banks," 26